Grandma's Tamales

*This book is dedicated to Abuelita.
Thank you for the precious memories
that you have given me.
I love you, Alyse*

**Written and photographed by
Donna L. Cuevas Roeder**

Today, Grandma is teaching me how to make tamales. First, she puts the chicken in a big pot to cook. Then, she separates the chicken from the bone to make the stuffing.

2

She then prepares the masa made of corn. She adds salt and other ingredients to make it taste good.

I begin to rinse and clean

the corn husks.

We sit down together and begin to spread the masa on the corn husks.

Then, we put the stuffing on top of the masa.

Grandma wraps them up and puts them in a big pot. Mmm! I wish that I could eat them right now!

Finally, the tamales are ready to eat. I love Grandma's tamales!